SELFLESS
IN A *Selfie*
WORLD

Before Honor is Humility

CODI GANDEE

WESTBOW®
PRESS
A DIVISION OF THOMAS NELSON
& ZONDERVAN

WestBow Press books may be ordered through booksellers or by contacting:

WestBow Press
A Division of Thomas Nelson & Zondervan
1663 Liberty Drive
Bloomington, IN 47403
www.westbowpress.com
1 (866) 928-1240

ISBN: 978-1-4908-6188-3 (sc)
ISBN: 978-1-4908-6187-6 (e)

Library of Congress Control Number: 2014921442

Printed in the United States of America.

WestBow Press rev. date: 12/5/2014

Contents

Acknowledgments

To my sister, Cassi McCoy, and sister-in-law, Kayla Hayhurst, thank you for giving your input from the very beginning. You were both so helpful to me throughout this process. Your feedback gave me courage to go on. I will be forever grateful.

To my very own cheerleaders: Sarah Dunkerson, Shannon Rushing, and Emma Rushing, thank you. You three women continually lifted me up in prayer and in encouraging words. Studying the Word with you is one of my favorite pastimes.

To Beth Eichelberger, my editor and friend, thank you. Your advice and input completed this study. I am now able to stand before the Lord completely confident that I have given my best work to Him.

And to Jesus, thank You. Not only have You redeemed me, but You have blessed me with the desires of my heart. I am so grateful for this opportunity.

Becoming a Christian

- First, you must realize that you are a sinner.
  "For all have sinned, and come short of the glory of God"
  (Rom. 3:23).

- And you must realize that there is a price for the sins you
  commit.
  "For the wages of sin is death; but the gift of God is eternal life
  through Jesus Christ our Lord" (Rom. 6:23).

- Then, understand that Jesus paid the price for your sins by
  dying on the cross and that He rose from the grave.
  "Who was delivered for our offenses, and was raised again for
  our justification" (Rom. 4:25).

- If you have accepted the fact that you are a sinner in need of a
  Savior, believe on Jesus to forgive you of your sins, and He will!
  "That if thou shalt confess with thy mouth The Lord Jesus, and
  shalt believe in thine heart that God hath raised him from the
  dead, thou shalt be saved" (Rom. 10:9).

  "For whosoever shall call upon the name of The Lord shall be
  saved" (Rom. 10:13).

- Get to know Jesus! Study the Word, the Bible.
  "In the beginning was the Word and the Word was with God,
  and the Word was God" (John 1:1).

- Choose each day from here on out to live for Jesus.

  "I am crucified with Christ: nevertheless I live; yet not I, but Christ liveth in me: and the life which I now live in the flesh I live by the faith of the Son of God, who loved me, and gave himself for me" (Gal. 2:20).

- Enjoy God's love!

  "We love him, because he first loved us" (1 John 4:19).

A Letter from the Author

About fifteen years ago, I surrendered to the call of teaching God's Word. I have enjoyed it ever since. I just think it is so amazing what God has for His children at their fingertips!

Throughout most of that time, I taught classes of every age, from young to old. But then we moved to a new area, and my opportunities to teach dwindled.

It was then that the Lord called me to teach via the blog leavingalegacyministries.com. This website I created has given me a platform to encourage Christians from all over the world. I am so very grateful for this opportunity!

But gradually I felt the Lord calling me to reach out in a different way. I wanted to encourage others to get into their Bibles and allow God to speak to them. The intimate, personal relationship that I have with Jesus surpasses anything in my life that I've ever known. I wanted others to become "hooked," too. Study guides are the perfect tool to promote a relationship with Christ that includes opening the Word and meditating on it daily. Writing study guides became the desire of my heart.

All I needed was God's approval and willingness to bless it.

One Sunday morning while in worship service, my "wants" evolved into a responsibility. After months of prayer, the Lord gave me

Scripture and reassurance that He wanted me to go forth with the ideas He had placed in my heart. I sat in service with tears streaming down my face, hands held high, and committed myself to the call of creating Bible studies to be used as a tool to help people grow in Jesus.

The following year became one of the most hectic years of my life. Our oldest child was beginning kindergarten. My dad had unexpected open-heart surgery. My husband began pastoring a new church. And at least one of the five of us was sick seemingly nonstop.

It was during these times that I felt like giving up on the study or at the very minimum postponing it. I was reminded, though, that we don't serve God when it's convenient for us. We are to serve the Lord no matter what our situation may be.

So, through the strength of God—because, let me tell you, I was weak—I pressed on. And here you are. God has something special for you as you complete this study. You just might be the very reason the Lord laid this on my heart.

I hope that you enjoy it. But even more than that, I pray that you grow in the grace and knowledge of our Lord and Savior Jesus Christ.

A Guide to the Guide

This study is broken into sixteen lessons within four chapters. You should complete the lessons in numerical order. At the end of each chapter, there is an opportunity to meet with others who are also completing the study.

The purposes of the meetings are:

- to give opportunity for Christians to gather together and talk about Jesus;
- to be encouraged that other Christians are studying their Bible and trying to live according to it;
- to strengthen relationships with other Christians; and
- to discuss and learn with others.

It isn't necessary that you do this study as part of a group. That being said, I do encourage you to become part of one. The Word teaches us that "iron sharpenth iron; so a man sharpeneth the countenance of his friend" (Pro. 27:17) meaning it's a good thing to fellowship with and be held accountable by other followers of Christ.

I also encourage you to pray before you begin each lesson. Then, worship Jesus, if for no other reason than He saved your soul. Dive into the Word with an open heart, willing to learn what the Spirit has to teach you.

Introduction

In contrast to a world that pushes you to promote yourself above all others, the doctrine of Christ teaches humility. Followers of Jesus are taught to be reverent to a sovereign God, to exalt one another, and to be servants to those around them. Not only does God delight in His people's humility, but He will bless them for it.

Throughout this study, we are going to learn how to be the humble people that God desires us to be. We will be studying several characters throughout the Word in hopes of gaining an understanding of what God wants for His people.

I encourage you to pray and meditate upon the Word and its truths as the Spirit reveals them to you. You have been given the opportunity to lead a more fulfilling, fruit-producing life. Enjoy what God has in store for you.

Chapter 1

Following in Jesus' Footsteps

We should live humbly because Jesus lived humbly. Philippians 2:5 says, "Let this mind be in you which was also in Christ Jesus."

Jesus Christ is our ultimate example for every aspect of our lives. This includes our lifestyle choices. He chose, while He sat on His heavenly throne being worshipped by angels, to come to this earth He had created. His choice at that moment was the beginning of the most humble act ever taken. From then on, He lived a life in which each choice He made benefited us, His creation. We are going to study one of the toughest choices He made: the decision to go through with His crucifixion.

LESSON 1

Let's begin with a definition.
Humility: The quality or condition of being humble.[1]

Okay, so let's move on to the definition of humble.
Humble: Having or showing a modest or low estimate of one's own importance. [2]

---

[1] Accessed online at http://dictionary.reference.com/browse/humility?s=t
[2] Accessed online at http://www.oxforddictionaries.com/us/definition/american_english/humble

So, how can modest be defined?

Modest: Unassuming or moderate in the estimation of one's abilities or achievements.[3]

Humility can be summed up as follows: Humility is when a person is humble. And a person who is humble chooses to rely on somebody else for success. Please read the following Scripture passages and answer the questions that follow.

- Matthew 16:24
  Who is being denied?

- Matthew 16:24
  Who is being followed?

Without Jesus and His humility, no heavenly reward or earthly blessings of worth could be obtained. All of the people who follow Jesus as their Redeemer, guide, and example need to at least have a foundation in humility.

Our Christian walk is rooted in humility. Throughout this study, we will learn how to grow in it. We will begin by looking to Jesus. His example is always the best place to start. We'll be studying the passage of Scripture found in Philippians 2:1–11 to better understand Jesus' humble walk. We will also be using this text as the base for our entire study.

---

[3] Accessed online athttp://www.oxforddictionaries.com/definition/english/modest

Three Parts of Humility:

- Trust
- Exaltation
- Servanthood

Text: Philippians 2:1-11

Seek and Find

- Philippians 2:1

When we first humbly came to Jesus, we completely trusted Him for salvation. List what else we can trust Him for.

- Philippians 2:3
  How are we supposed to view others?

- Philippians 2:4
  Are we supposed to help each other? Why?

- Philippians 2:5
  After whom should we model our way of thinking?

- Philippians 2:7
  What role did Jesus take on when He submitted to the cross?

- Philippians 2:8
  What did Jesus do to prepare for the cross?

- Philippians 2:9
  How did God reward Jesus?

Think about It

- Pride could have ruled Jesus' decision when it was time to choose if He was willing to die for us. But He didn't allow pride to rule. Instead, He chose to see our need for a perfect sacrifice as more worthy than His life; He exalted us. He chose to give Himself, even though we could never repay Him; He served us. And He did all of this because He believed that His Father's plan was best; He trusted God. Jesus giving His life on the cross of Calvary is the picture of humility. Based on Jesus' example, describe the three parts of humility.
  1.
  2.
  3.

Wrapping It Up

Jesus is to be every Christian's role model. He is the one that we are to look to for every answer in our lives. Just as He is perfect in every way so was His humility. Jesus was the epitome of humility as He lived life, gave His life in death, and became our risen Savior. He is the reason why we Christians should strive to be a humble people.

MEETING 1

- Begin in prayer.
- Have each person share a personal, most favorite God moment.
- Then silently read the story below.

Where will pride get you? In the middle of a field, roaming around with mental issues for seven years if you're like King Nebuchadnezzar.

You see, Daniel had interpreted a dream of despair to the king. He had told him that he would hit rock bottom and stay there until he realized that the magnificence of his kingdom was from God and not himself.

Eight years later, King Nebuchadnezzar was standing in the middle of a field, looking and acting like a wild man, when he acknowledged God's presence in his life, in his success.

It wasn't until after this proclamation of praise and honor to our King that he was given back his kingdom.

I encourage you to learn from King Nebuchadnezzar and give God glory now so that you won't have to be reminded that He is the one that is worthy of all your praise—because the proud will be humbled, and the humble will be honored.

Answer the following questions for your own use. Keep this just between you and Jesus.

○   If you could overhear a conversation in which you were the main topic, what would you hope to hear being said about you?

○   What do you think Jesus would want to have said about you?

○   Do you believe that you are capable of being humble?

○   Do you try to lift up other people?

○   Do you serve those around you?

- Discuss the encouragement that you've gained from Jesus' humble walk.
- Discuss the encouragement that you've gained from one another.
- Take the opportunity to praise each other, remarking on something positive in the lives of those among you.
- End in prayer.

Chapter 2

Making the Cut: No One Is Exempt from Being Humble

Do you trust that God wants what is best for you? Philippians 2:1–2 says, "If there be any consolation in Christ, if any comfort of love, if any fellowship of the Spirit, if any bowels and mercies, fulfill ye my joy, that ye be likeminded, having the same love, being of one accord, of one mind."

This chapter focuses on you. The goal of these lessons is to teach you that regardless of your past, Jesus wants your future. A future with Jesus is always blessed. Throughout the next few lessons, we'll study how none of these people were exempt from leading a humble life, even though they all came from different backgrounds. Jesus had the best intentions for them, just as He does for you.

An Answered Prayer

So, it was the beginning of a new school year, and I was picking up my daughter on one of the first days. We were new to the area. I had dressed myself in a super cute outfit; I wanted to give a "blessed" impression to the community of parents and teachers.

Now know that this pickup process wasn't really all that involved. I just had to wait my turn in the long line of other parents, drive to the front door, hop out, get my daughter, and buckle her in.

My turn had come around. Now was my chance to make an impression on these people. I saw my daughter standing at the door. I jumped out to go meet her. And then the unthinkable happened: my shoe broke. No, this story is not quite as dramatic as I have led you to believe, but it was still devastating to me in that moment. I tried to recover quickly, act nonchalant, and just slide it along. No way was I wanting to stoop down, retrieve my broken shoe, and walk barefoot back to my vehicle. But that's exactly what I had to do. With my shoe in one hand and my daughter's hand in the other, I hobbled back to my car embarrassed.

It was then that my prayer from earlier that day came back to me: "Lord, make me humble. I don't know much about humility besides the fact that proud people fall. I don't want to take my family down with me, so please, humble me now."

Now I don't believe that God tore my sandal apart out of anger. But I knew that there was a lesson to be learned from the pickup incident. I just didn't have any idea what it was. Compelled to learn about humility, I began to dig into the subject to find out what it actually meant to be humble.

LESSON 2

By studying just a portion of Jesus' walk, as recorded in Philippians, we have learned that we should be humble. But the Word goes beyond just giving us the picture of humility. It also tells us why we need to strive for humility.

Seek and Find

Please read the following Scripture passages and answer the questions that follow:

- Psalm 131:1

  David, a man after God's own heart, refers to himself as being humble when speaking with the Lord. It seems as if David is pleading his case with God, almost as if he is trying to convey to Him that he has tried so diligently to be humble. What does this tell us about humility? Circle the correct answer below.

    a. Humility just happens.
    b. Humble is something that you have to be determined to become.

- John 2:16

  True or false: Lust and pride are things of the world. Therefore, humility must be of God.

- Psalm 86:11

  Who is capable of teaching us godly attributes?

- Psalm 86:11

  If we have to be taught how to be humble, then we can't accidentally humble ourselves. How will this help us to become more humble? Circle the correct answer below.

    - We are aware of our humility.
    - We are aware of our lack of humility and how much we have to learn.
    - Both A and B.

- Isaiah 57:15
  According to this Scripture, what type of a person will live for eternity with Jesus?

- James 4:10
  How will the Lord respond to a humble person?

- Proverbs 29:23
  How does being a humble person affect your witness?

- Proverbs 22:4
  In addition to standing with the Lord, growing in Him, and being a good witness in front of our peers, how else do we benefit from humility?

God wants you to walk humbly to be able to receive all of humility's benefits. He loves you and wants the best for you. You have to believe that. You have to trust Him. You have to know that He has your best interest in mind. Please read the following Scripture passages and answer the questions that follow:

- Jeremiah 31:3
  Jesus created you in love. What does that tell you about the relationship that He wants to have with you?

- John 3:16
  Jesus gave His life on the cross of Calvary. What does this mean to you?

- Jeremiah 29:11
  How does the Lord reassure you with this Scripture?

Think about It

- Why is humility something that you have to be aware of doing?

- List what the benefits of being humble are.

- How do you know that Jesus has chosen you to be a humble person?

Wrapping It Up

God's greatest blessings begin with humility. From the very beginning of our Christian walk, He taught us to rely on Him for salvation, not ourselves. Now we see all of the other benefits that come from being a humble person of God. God only has the best intentions in mind for you. He wants you to serve Him and live in a way that will give you great joy. Take Jesus up on His offer and intentionally make your journey clothed in humility.

LESSON 3

The previous study taught us about our importance to God and how much He desires for us to be humble. He loves us, has a plan for us, and wants us to walk uprightly in Him, aware of our actions. Because of this, we can conclude that even in the worst circumstances, God still wants us to follow Him. No matter what our past or current position is, He can turn it to good.

Today we will be studying about how Joash, a boy who had been born into a wicked family in a dire situation, was able to live humbly before the Lord.

Text: 2 Chronicles chapters 21–24

Seek and Find

- 2 Chronicles 21:4
  Jehoram, Joash's *grandfather*, did what to try to secure his kingdom?

- 2 Chronicles 22:4
  What type of a king was Ahaziah, Joash's *father?*

- 2 Chronicles 22:9
  What happened to Joash's father, Ahaziah?

This opened the throne to Joash's uncles, brothers, and cousins.

- 2 Chronicles 22:10
  How did Joash's *grandmother*, Athaliah, react to her son's death?

- 2 Chronicles 22:11
  One baby escaped, Athaliah's grandson. What was his name?

Fill in the Blank.

Describe each person in Joash's family tree with one word.

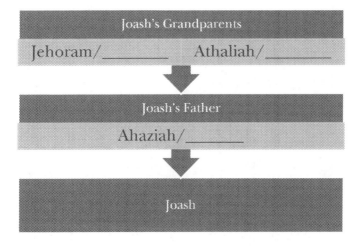

- 2 Chronicles 22:11

  Joash was saved by his father's sister, Jehoshabeath. Who was she married to?

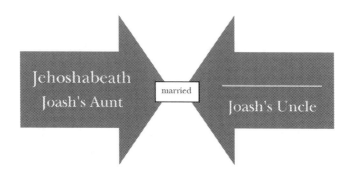

- 2 Chronicles 22:12

  How many years was Joash hidden from Athaliah?

- 2 Chronicles 23:16

  How was Jehoiada influential in restoring Judah back to a nation that served the Lord?

- 2 Chronicles 24:1

  Joash began his reign as king of Judah at what age?

- 2 Chronicles 23:13
  What was Athaliah's reaction to Joash becoming king?

- 2 Chronicles 23:15
  What happened to Athaliah?

- 2 Chronicles 24:2
  What type of influence did Jehoiada have on Joash's life?

- 2 Chronicles 24:4
  What did God allow Joash to accomplish during his reign?

- 2 Chronicles 24:14
  Were Joash, Jehoiada, and the Israelites successful in serving God?

Think about It

- What type of a situation had Joash been born into?

- When Joash first began his reign as king, why did his future look so bleak?

- Even though the odds of Joash becoming a godly ruler looked grim, there was still hope. Why was Jehoiada's role so crucial in the life of Joash?

- Just when it appeared that things couldn't get any worse for Joash, his grandmother Athaliah, tried for a second time to have him killed. Again Jehoiada stepped in to defend Joash and ultimately regained the kingdom on Joash's behalf. How do you think that Joash felt toward his uncle?

- These feelings led Joash to esteem Jehoiada above everyone else in his life. His exaltation of Jehoiada led him to a walk in a way that would also exalt God. He was a humble man because he esteemed his uncle Jehoiada. During the time that Joash reigned as a humble leader, was he blessed?

Wrapping It Up

God kept Joash alive because He had a plan for him. It didn't matter that Joash was only seven years old when he took over the kingdom. And it doesn't matter how old you are now or what kind of past you may have had. You are here because God has a plan for you. He loved you even when He brought you into a world of darkness. God placed someone in Joash's life—his aunt and uncle—to lead him to the Lord. He has given you someone too, perhaps the person who suggested that you do this study.

LESSON 4

This lesson is going to focus on a common man, born into a common situation, yet he was called to do mighty things. God was able to use him when he humbled himself before the Lord.

Text: Judges chapter 6

Seek and Find

- Judges 6:11
  What was Gideon doing when an angel met him for the first time?

- Judges 6:12
  The angel referred to Gideon as what type of a person?

- Judges 6:13, 15
  How did Gideon respond to the angel?

- Judges 6:14
  What did God choose Gideon to do?

- Judges 6:16
  Gideon was sketchy about accepting the call. How did God comfort him?

- Judges 6:36–40; 7:9–11, 15
  Gideon had several emotions overcome him. What were some of them?

Think about It

- Surely if you had been given the choice to select a leader of an army, you wouldn't have chosen Gideon. Even Gideon himself wouldn't have chosen Gideon. Why do you think that was?

Through Gideon's conversation with the angel, we learn a couple things about Gideon's background:

> - 1) The Israelites had been hiding in captivity for years. This information tells us that Gideon didn't have any experience in warfare.

- **2)** He was the least of his brethren. Now we know that he lacked in leadership abilities also.

- God called Gideon a brave man, even though he was hiding from his captors when the angel first met with him. How does this show us that God always has our future in mind?

- Gideon realized that he was the servant and that God was the one in charge. In our first lesson, we learned that servanthood is humility in action. Pride would have been the only factor that could have caused Gideon to forsake God's plan to go with his own. Why wouldn't he have been successful?

Wrapping It Up

Gideon was just an ordinary man. He was just like any other Israelite at that time. He feared the Midianites. He didn't have any prior warfare or leadership experience. Yet God chose Gideon to lead the nation of Israel away from idol worship and into freedom from the Midianites. Gideon's normalcy or lack of qualifications didn't deter God from using him to do great things. Gideon's humility was what allowed him to be a successful leader.

LESSON 5

In the previous lessons of this chapter, we have studied the situations that men were born into. This study is a bit different because the man we will be studying wasn't born into a grand situation; he was grafted into it. Let's take a look at how Jonathan responded humbly to being given a cushy position in life.

Text: 1 Samuel chapters 9–23

Seek and Find

- 1 Samuel 9:21
  Who was Saul?

- 1 Samuel 11:15
  What status was Saul elevated to?

- 1 Samuel 14:49
  Who was Jonathan's father?

- 1 Samuel 16:13
  Who was anointed to be the next king in line for Saul's throne?

- 1 Samuel 18:1
  What were Jonathan's feelings toward David?

- 1 Samuel 19:5
  At what point did Jonathan recognize God's favor on David?

- 1 Samuel 18:4
  What items did Jonathan give to David?

- 1 Samuel 19:1, 4
  Jonathan knew of Saul's plan to kill David. How did he react?

- 1 Samuel 23:16–17
  Did Jonathan have any hard feelings toward David for taking his inheritance from him?

- 2 Samuel 9:6–7
  How was Jonathan blessed for his humility?

Think about It

- 1 Samuel 18:1
  Jonathan was at an age that he understood what was happening when his father accepted the role as king of Israel. He witnessed firsthand the luxurious lifestyle that came with ruling a kingdom. He also saw the stark contrasts to the previous life he lived. He most likely thought about what this meant for him as heir. What type of an effect does that sudden change in social status usually have on a person?

- 1 Samuel 18:4
  Jonathan recognized the favor God had for David, and still there was an unbreakable bond between the men. This bond was only possible because of the absence of Jonathan's pride. He also esteemed David. How did Jonathan's gifts to David signify this?

- 1 Samuel 19:1, 4
  Jonathan wasn't just compliant to God's will in turning over the kingdom to David. He also played an important role in making it become reality. He proactively did everything within his power to make it happen. How so?

- 2 Samuel 9:6–7
  Jonathan's humility was rewarded with a legacy that he left for his descendants. In what ways was this blessing better

than the earthly gain that could have been his had he gone against God's will and become king of Israel?

Wrapping It Up

Jonathan was put into a position in which he could have very easily become haughty and high-minded. He could have focused on living for himself without regard to God's will or others. But he didn't. Instead, he chose to follow God's will, even though it excluded him from receiving the throne. He humbly submitted to God's plan and did everything within his power to make sure that it happened. God blessed Jonathan's humility by giving him a wonderful legacy and by blessing his descendants.

LESSON 6

Review of the Facts

Match the background with each character.

Joash   Prosperous

Jonathan   Terrible

Gideon   Common

Did Joash's age stop him from becoming king?

Did Gideon's lack of military experience keep him from becoming the general to lead a nation?

Jonathan stood to gain the kingdom. But instead, he chose to take a backseat to David. When viewed through worldly eyes, wasn't Jonathan the one suited best to rule the kingdom?

So, we have a seven-year-old king, a farmer for a general, and a prince who helped another man inherit his throne. None of these men followed in line with the standards of our world. But God was able to use them just as they were for His and their greatest glory.

Making It Applicable

What type of background do you have?

How has your background shaped your relationship with Jesus?

Have you allowed feelings of inadequacy or pride to deter you from pursuing God's will of humility for your life? Based on these past few studies, should you?

Do you deem yourself as qualified to be a humble person?

MEETING 2

- Open in prayer.
- Discuss *Review of the Facts* from Lesson 6.
- Read or give a summary of *An Answered Prayer.*

So, what did I learn from the pickup incident?

I failed, miserably. I was willing to allow my background to dictate my future. I was leaning on nice clothes, a good hair day, and a seemingly great pair of shoes to qualify me for a "blessed" status. I was focused on earthly qualifications instead of allowing the light within me to shine for Jesus. I had no intention of being a blessing to someone else. I was concerned with only me.

Thankfully, I learned from the experience. What was in my past didn't negatively affect my future with God. He can take any person out of whatever situation he or she is in and turn it for his or her good. Also, what is in my past doesn't give me a leg up on my future with God. His redeeming blood is still the only covering for my sin. The package I am when God receives me as His own is exactly what He uses for the building of His kingdom. He grows me into what He wants me to be through His mercy and grace.

Open up discussion between you and God and your brothers and sisters in Christ.

- Talk about the different types of backgrounds you've come from.
- Discuss how the Lord has taken what you thought of as stumbling blocks and used them as building blocks for the upbuilding of His kingdom.
- Encourage one another.
- Ask the Lord to show you how He can use your situations for His good.
- Close in prayer.

Chapter 3

Primed and Ready:
Examples in Exaltation

Do You Look to Exalt Others?

"Let nothing be done through strife or vainglory; but in lowliness of mind let each esteem other better than themselves" (Phil. 2:3).

In this chapter we will be studying exaltation. We will study how all personality types are capable of exalting others and some of the different approaches to exaltation.

A Humble Deacon

My heart was full of joy as my husband relayed the conversation that he had with a deacon of the church that we were currently attending.

"He recommended that they take me into consideration for their church's pastor. He said that he hated to see us leave, but that he felt like he would be doing wrong by blocking opportunities for us to serve the Lord if he didn't give the recommendation."

We had been attending church with this man for the past couple of years. We considered him to be part of our "family away from family." He and his wife cared for our children on occasion. We were neighbors. We studied the Word together. We had a great relationship with these friends sent to us straight from God.

So we weren't surprised or upset that he was willingly opening up doors for us to leave the church. We would have expected nothing less from this man of God. Our deacon had put the will of our Father above his own desires so that God would be glorified.

We were, and continue to be, so grateful for his expression of exaltation. This deacon's uplifting words came at a crucial time. They afforded us the opportunity to serve Jesus in the calling that had been placed on our hearts.

As a result, my husband is now serving as pastor in that neighboring church. We feel so much peace in this decision and God's sovereign hand upon us.

LESSON 7

In this lesson, we'll study how exaltation of others benefits you and what the Word says about exalting yourself.

Let's begin with a couple of definitions.

Esteem:

1. To respect or admire.[4]

---

[4] Accessed online at http://www.oxforddictionaries.com/definition/english/esteem

Exalt:

1. To hold someone in very high regard; think or speak highly of.
2. To raise in rank, character, or status; elevate.[5]

So basically, *exaltation* is what you should do when you *esteem* someone. *Exaltation* is like the action word for *esteem*.

- Characteristics you want to *avoid* when trying to live a humble life by exalting others:
  - *Living for you*
    - 1 Corinthians 10:33
      According to Paul, we should live our lives in a way that who is profited?

  - *Self-boasting*
    - Proverbs 27:2
      Who should praise you?

  - *Doing to be seen*
    - Matthew 6:1
      Should you do works of the Lord only to be seen by men?

---

[5] Accessed online at http://www.oxforddictionaries.com/definition/english/exalt

Exaltation of Others Replaces Self-Boasting

God is so good to us. When we follow the commandments that God has given, we are replacing the opportunity to be disobedient. When we are consumed with exalting others, we are unconcerned with self-boasting. This not only benefits your walk with Jesus, but it also benefits those around you.

- Luke 14:7–11
  - Where was the man told to sit?

  - Why was he told to sit there?

  - How was he exalting others by choosing a lower seat for himself?

  - When he chose to sit in the lower seat, it took away the opportunity for people to accuse him of being what?

God's wisdom is unlike man's, but that is such a wonderful truth. The concept that He gives—"humble yourself and you will be exalted"—is contradictory to common sense, yet it is completely true. We see it play out again and again throughout the Scriptures.

"Humble yourselves therefore under the mighty hand of God, that he may exalt you in due time" (1 Peter 5:6).

LESSON 8

In this lesson, we will be studying about John, Jesus' first cousin. He accepted the role as Jesus' forerunner and dedicated his life to exalting Christ. We will study John's personality and his approach to being humble.

Text: Matthew chapter 3

Seek and Find

- Matthew 3:3
  John linked himself to Jesus. What did he say he was there to do for the Lord?

- Matthew 3:4
  What did John wear?

- Matthew 3:4
  What types of food did he eat?

- Matthew 3:1, 6

  What did John do?

- Matthew 3:7–9

  How did John speak to the Pharisees and Sadducees?

- Matthew 3:13

  Who came to John to be baptized?

- Matthew 3:15–16

  John didn't exactly agree that he should be the one to baptize Jesus. But Jesus told him that it was necessary. Did John comply with Jesus' will?

Think about It

- Considering the type of clothes that John wore, the food that he ate, and the lifestyle that he lived, what type of personality would you say that he had? Circle the correct answer below.

    a. reserved

    b. eccentric

    c. timid

- The boldness that John spoke with when talking to the Pharisees and Sadducees seemed a bit strong. But even in those statements, he was still humble because he was exalting God. He was trying to lift these people up, to lead these people to know the truth. Jesus knew the approach that John would take with these people, and yet He deemed him a humble man. Are people who are frank excluded from being humble?

- John's boldness almost landed him in trouble, though. The Bible reads as if he were very close to telling Jesus to go find someone else to baptize Him. But because he esteemed Christ above his own ideas, he listened to the plan that Christ had for him. Obviously John didn't want to baptize Jesus. Why do you think that was? Circle the correct answer below.
    a. He felt unworthy.
    b. He was uninterested.
    c. He didn't feel he had time.

- In reality, none of us is worthy to do anything for Christ until He changes us. Once we become His, then our mind-set needs to change. If all Christians walked around declining callings of the Lord citing unworthiness, then the Gospel wouldn't spread very far. In addition to unworthiness, what are some other reasons that people use to not do the will of God?

A common reason to shy away from doing the work of the Lord is: "*I don't want to draw attention to myself.*"

Let's look at how the baptism of Jesus would have gone if no one had been willing to baptize our Lord.

- ○ Jesus wouldn't have been baptized!
- ○ He wouldn't have had the dove (representing the Spirit of God) descend upon Him.
- ○ God wouldn't have had the opportunity to announce Him as His son.

So, while the "I don't want to receive attention" may sound humble, it isn't if it goes against God's plan.

Notice also that in the end, the baptism really wasn't about John. I doubt anyone walked away from the baptism saying, "Boy, did you see John take him under like that? That guy has a real talent for baptizing people." Instead, the baptism focused on Christ. Everyone there was caught up with seeing the dove descend and hearing the voice of God from heaven. Just as Jesus received the glory in this situation, He will also receive the glory when we follow His will for us. We will be part of the picture, but the focus will be on Jesus.

- ○ **True or False:** A humble person will surrender to doing the will of the Lord regardless of attention that may or may not be gained and worthiness that may or may not be felt.

Wrapping It Up

John exalted Jesus in a way that was unique to his personality. He was eccentric. He was frank. But in all of this, he was humble. Because of his humbleness, we will forever remember John as a forerunner for Christ, the man who dedicated his entire life to seeing Jesus lifted up.

LESSON 9

In this lesson, we will be comparing and contrasting two men from the book of Esther. We will be studying Haman and Esther's adoptive father, Mordecai.

We will be studying their lives to see the direct effects of exalting others versus exalting one's self. Also, we will see how it isn't always a bad thing to include others in your acts of humility.

Text: Esther chapters 2–8

Seek and Find

Neither Received the Recognition Deserved

Mordecai is best known as the uncle of Queen Esther, but before she became queen he was already "sitting in the king's gate." He is serving in this position in the following scriptures:

(Esther 2:21-22) What does Mordecai report?

(Esther 6:3) What type of recognition had Mordecai received up to that point?

Despite adversity, Mordecai didn't leave the king's courts—he carried on.

> **Haman is a man that has recently received a promotion above all of the princes.**
>
> (Esther 3:2) Haman is promoted to one of the chief men, and people are told to bow to him. Who chooses to not bow to Haman?
>
>
> (Esther 3:6) How did Haman want to handle this?

Who did Haman want to please when he came up with his plan? Circle the correct answer below.

    a.   himself

    b.   the king

Whose well-being was at the forefront of Mordecai's mind? Circle the correct answer below.

    a.   his own

    b.   the king's

Who was involved in the hanging of the potential assassins? Circle the correct answer below.

    a.   just Mordecai

    b.   Mordecai, the queen, the king, and the people who built the gallows

Conversing With Others

Mordecai has just received word that the Jews are to be destroyed and is very distraught. He goes into mourning, tearing his clothes, wearing ashes, and wailing in the street. Queen Esther sends a chamberlain to check on him, opening the door for Mordecai to speak directly with the queen. This is how the conversation, via the chamberlain, plays out:

(Esther 4:8) What did Mordecai urge Esther to do?

(Esther 4:15-17) Mordecai then went to the Jewish people of Shushan. What did he ask them to do?

Haman has recently been given a promotion within the kingdom. He has just received word that he is to attend a banquet in which only he, the king, and the queen will attend. This is how Haman chooses to spend his time leading up to the event:

(Esther 5:10) What did he do when he arrived home?

(Esther 5:11-13) What two topics were discussed?

    1.

    2.

(Esther 5:14) Who was Haman looking to please?

Esther 5:14 What does he decide to do about it?

Who was Mordecai concerned about when communicating with the queen? Circle the correct answer below.

    a.   the Jews

    b.   himself

Who was Haman concerned with promoting while visiting with his company? Circle the correct answer below.

    a.   himself

    b.   his guests

Both Men Go Before the King

The king has just read of Mordecai's heroic act of foiling the plan of the would-be murderers. He is looking to honor Mordecai. He would like some advice on how to properly do this, so he calls for Haman.

(Esther 6:6) Who does Haman think that the "man to be honored" is?

(Esther 6:8-9) What does Haman suggest be done?

Mordecai has received favor from the king and has been given a promotion. He is now presiding over the princes that Haman once reigned over and stands before the king.

(Esther 8:8) What did the king give Mordecai permission to do?

(Esther 8:11) What type of law did Mordecai write?

Mordecai was given the spotlight. Whom did he look to exalt? Circle the correct answer below.

    a.   himself

    b.   his people

How was Mordecai able to encourage the Jewish people? Circle the correct answer below.

    a.   He went and spoke to each of them.

    b.   He spoke with Queen Esther's chamberlain, who then took the message to the queen, who then went to the king, and the king then allowed Mordecai to write a new decree to be published through the land.

Esther 10:3

How was Mordecai's humility rewarded? Circle the correct answer below.

    a.   death

    b.   promotion

Think about It

Fill in the Blank with *Methodical* or *Normal*

Mordecai was a _____ man. He served daily as a king's servant, just the same as many others.

Mordecai could be called _____ because he used the queen's influence on the king to save a nation of people.

Wrapping It Up

Mordecai was an ordinary guy who chose to become a positive influence in the lives of others. He chose to humble himself and fight for the king and his nation. He did this even though it meant he had to go through different people to get the results he was after. In all his efforts to save the people around him, he never looked for self-promotion. He was a direct contrast to Haman and his worldly wisdom. The ends of their lives sum up for us why it is most beneficial for us to exalt others and not self-promote. Mordecai was given the position of the king's right hand man, and Haman was hung.

We learn from Mordecai's example that sometimes it is necessary for us to go through others to exalt people who are in need. Involving others in our humility isn't always a bad thing. Sometimes it is required, as it was in Mordecai's case.

LESSON 10

In this lesson, we will be studying about two timid men, Joseph and Nicodemus. These men thought very highly of Jesus. They thought highly enough of Him to exalt Jesus in His death.

Text: John 19:30–42

Seek and Find

- John 19:38
  Joseph of Arimathaea was a disciple of whom?

- John 19:38
  In what manner did Joseph approach Pilate?

- John 19:38
  What did Joseph want from Pilate?

- John 19:39
  Who helped Joseph?

- John 19:39
  At what time of day did Nicodemus come to Jesus?

- John 19:40
  How did they prepare the body of Jesus?

- John 19:41–42
  What did they do with Jesus' body?

Think about It

- Besides the Bible plainly stating that Joseph was a follower of Jesus, what are some other clues that jump out at you?

- Joseph seemed bent on getting Jesus buried fast. Pilate wasn't even certain that Jesus had actually died when he was approached by Joseph. Why is immediate obedience important, especially for a timid person?

- Shy, scared, or timid people tend to need extra encouragement. Nicodemus, a seemingly timid person himself, was available and willing to help Joseph. What do you think this did for Joseph? Could you be a "Nicodemus" to someone?

- There were a few burial rituals that had to take place. The spices and the wrapping of the body were needful. Even though these men were trying to be secretive, the Bible is very clear that Jesus received the proper burial. This speaks volumes about Joseph and Nicodemus. It shows us that they were able to get past their fleshly concerns to exalt Jesus' life in caring for Him in His death.

Wrapping It Up

Joseph and Nicodemus come across as timid men. They didn't allow this personality trait to hinder them in exalting Jesus. They esteemed Him so much that they took the opportunity to humble themselves before God and care for His son's body. In secret, they exalted Christ. But they were blessed publicly. Forever they will be in Scripture as men who craved Jesus more than their own life.

LESSON 11

Review of the Facts

Match the type of personality to each character.

John   Timid

Mordecai   Eccentric

Joseph and Nicodemus   Average

Match the approach of exaltation used by each character.

John   Secretive

Mordecai   Help to Others

Joseph and Nicodemus   Frankness

Making It Applicable

What type of personality do you have?

Have you ever excused yourself from being humble because of your personality?

What approach do you tend toward most often?

What truth has Jesus revealed to you in these past few studies?

How have you esteemed Jesus over yourself?

MEETING 3

- Open in prayer.
- Discuss *Review of the Facts* from Lesson 11.
- Summarize *A Humble Deacon*.

As I listened to my husband relay the facts of our situation, I knew we were being blessed. I didn't grasp the magnitude at the time. It was only after studying the Word that I realized the effort our deacon put forth to see God glorified. He was willing to enlist the help of others to see us lifted up. He chose to allow his personality to work for the glory of God instead of against it. God used this humble man as part of the plan He had for my life. For that, I am very grateful.

Open up discussion between you and God and your brothers and sisters in Christ.

- Discuss how different personalities can lead some to think that they are exempt from being humble.
- Discuss common approaches to exalting others.
- Encourage one another.
- Give God praise.
- Close with prayer.

Chapter 4

Game Time: The Know-How's of Servanthood

Do You Serve Those around You?

"Look not every man on his own things, but every man also on the things of others" (Phil. 2:4).

So far we've studied who is called to be humble, what types of personalities are capable of being humble, and some different ways in which people can exalt others.

In this chapter we will be studying three different people from the Bible. Each of these people chose to serve another person. The methods in which they served and the frequency of their servanthood is the basis of this chapter.

Cold Feet

On Easter morning, my family and I were traveling to church for sunrise service. Given the time of day (at least we'll blame it on that), I forgot to make sure that both of my girls had socks on with their pajamas. Twenty minutes later, my younger daughter began to complain that her feet were cold.

My solution: sit on them.

My six-year-old's response: she took her socks off and gave them to her sister.

I was so blessed by this act of humility.

She thought more of her sister's comfort than she did her own—so much more that she was willing to sacrifice cozy feet so that her sister's would no longer be cold.

Given that you don't have the same ties to my children as I do, you may not be as moved by this story. Maybe you're thinking, "Come on really, you were *driving* to church. And you're talking about comfort, not necessity. Some people are far worse off."

I understand that. But I want you to see it as God did: sacrificial love.

LESSON 12

In this lesson, we are going to be gaining the foundation for why we should serve. Throughout the Bible, serving seems to be a reoccurring theme. Again, if we go back to Jesus' sacrifice as recorded in Philippians, even He humbled himself to become a servant of God.

Since we are going to be focusing on servanthood, let's get a definition.

Serve:

1. To perform duties or services for.[6]

---

[6] Accessed online at http://www.oxforddictionaries.com/definition/english/serve

Servanthood:

1. The role of being a servant.[7]

How have you served others?

How do people within your community serve one another?

It seems as if most people are servants in one form or another. So the question then becomes: what separates God's servants from man's servants?

Circle the correct answer below.

Whose servant are you …

if you're serving others because your job requires it? **God or man**

if you're seeking an earthly reward? **God or man**

if you are serving others because you want to follow in Jesus' footsteps? **God or man**

if you are serving others because Christ served you? **God or man**

Read Luke 14:12–14.

---

[7] Accessed online at http://www.yourdictionary.com/servanthood

Circle the correct choices below.

The people here were opening their homes with what purpose in mind?

    a.   to feed the poor

    b.   to promote themselves

That was the game played within these social circles. It also sounds eerily similar to today's society. Who did Jesus tell them to feed?

    a.   the ones in need

    b.   the ones who were looking for self-gain

As Christ's followers, we want to take heed of this teaching. We should serve with the intention of glorifying God, not ourselves.

In the last chapter, we studied how John had to humble himself and exalt Jesus, even though in his flesh, he felt like he would be receiving too much attention. The same trap is often used in trying to discourage servanthood, too. We allow ourselves to believe that servanthood should only be done if absolutely no one will ever find out about it. This isn't true.

According to Matthew 6:1, the act of service becomes null and void in God's records when:

    a.   we make a big to-do and serve only with the intent of being seen by men.

    b.   the one being served appreciates the service.

The intentions of our heart should dictate our decision to serve or not to serve. If we are serving to glorify God, then by all means, please, I beg you, do it! However, if you're serving so that you will gain the rewards of man, resist the temptation. Pray for the desire of your heart to change. When you're serving with the intent of self-promotion, the only one truly being served is yourself. The others involved are just part of your plan.

Maybe you're concerned that someone might mistake your godly intentions as "seeking attention" or "being showy." According to 1 Peter 3:17, you should:

    a.   go on about the Father's service and take whatever criticism may come your way.

    b.   allow fear to freeze you dead in your tracks.

We must not fall into the trap of inactivity for Christ because of fear of man's perception of God's work in our life. Some people can take any good, God-glorifying act and put a terrible spin on it.

Be comforted, though. In Luke 8:17, the Bible teaches that the intents of our heart will:

    a.   be made known.

    b.   be brought to light.

    c.   both A and B

Isn't it fascinating how the teachings of the Word of God go against the wisdom of this world? For example:

- Proverbs 22:9
  According to this Scripture, what is a sure way to be blessed? Circle the correct answer below.
    a. Keep all blessings to yourself.
    b. Help those in need.

- Luke 6:35
  In this self-serving, "I'm looking out for number one" world, the common belief is to promote yourself above all others, using whomever you can along the way. This Scripture tells us that we shouldn't bless people just to gain a reward from them in return. Instead, this Scripture teaches that we should serve people with the hope of receiving a reward from whom?

Fill in the Blank with *Others* or *Ourselves*

- 1 Corinthians 10:33
  Paul teaches here that our main concern shouldn't be for _____. Instead, our main concern should be for _____.

Wrapping It Up

The act of servanthood, with the intent of serving Jesus first and foremost, may never become habit to you. Even if that is the case, I encourage you to continue to put forth the effort to humble yourself so that Jesus' name and kingdom will be lifted up. The sacrifice of service will benefit all those involved: Jesus, others, and you.

Enter into servanthood joyfully. It is a vital part of humility. It was the necessary route for Jesus to take to prepare a gateway into heaven. Through servanthood, you are worshipping your Savior by clinging to His promises and putting into practice His teachings. The blessings of humility will be your reward.

LESSON 13

In this lesson, we are going to be studying about Philip and the importance of humble living without regard to our fleshly way of thinking.

Text: Acts 8:26–40

Seek and Find

According to Acts 8:26:

- Philip was told to go down to Gaza, which was near which city?

- What type of climate did Gaza have? Circle the correct answer below.
  - cool and damp
  - hot and dry

Acts 8:27
Who was traveling with Queen Candace?

Acts 8:28
What was he doing as he traveled home from Jerusalem?

Acts 8:29
What was Philip told to do?

Acts 8:30
What was Philip's response?

Acts 8:30
What did Philip say to the Ethiopian treasurer?

Acts 8:31
What did the treasurer ask Philip to do?

Acts 8:35
What did Philip do?

Acts 8:36
What did they pass in the desert?

Acts 8:36
What did the Ethiopian want to do?

Acts 8:38

What was Philip able to do for the treasurer?

Acts 8:39

What happened to Philip next?

Think about It

Circle the correct answer below.

We learned that Philip was immediately obedient to the angel of the Lord. Notice in the Scripture that it didn't mention what Philip was doing when the angel of the Lord spoke to him. It just said that Philip went. Perhaps this detail was omitted because:

    a.   it didn't compare to the task that Philip had before him.

    b.   the author forgot.

Philip understood that the things that he had been doing weren't of top priority, even though they very well may have been important. Since he stopped what he was doing to follow the will of God, we can conclude that Philip was:

    a.   humble.

    b.   proud.

Furthermore, Philip ran, in a desert, to meet the chariot. To me, this is the perfect showing of humility. I, for one, am not a runner. To run on a nice day in running clothes and shoes is too much for me.

But maybe Philip enjoyed running. Even so, he had to exert himself to meet the chariot in which the treasurer rode. The timing wasn't coincidental. It didn't "just so happen" that he would meet him as the Ethiopian was reading about Jesus' crucifixion. What does this say to us about our obedience to the Lord?

Another circumstance that was orchestrated by God was the placement of the water in the middle of a desert. How amazing to think that when God created the world, he knew that one day this Ethiopian man would dedicate his life to Him because of Jesus and then be baptized by Philip in this very pool of water. How did Philip's obedience affect the Ethiopian treasurer?

Does it pay to be humble or to live humbly in front of a person that you may see only one time?

Wrapping It Up

Being humble is of great importance, even if we think we might not be very effective. Philip could have denied the angel of the

Lord. He might have argued, "I don't go to Gaza very often. How can I have a positive effect on someone's life in one instance?"

We see that because Philip humbled himself and became obedient to God's will, he didn't just have a positive effect on a person, but even greater: a man's place in eternity was forever changed.

LESSON 14

In this lesson, we will be studying about a woman who humbled herself in spite of her financial circumstances to make a difference in another person's life.

According to Proverbs 22:9, generous people are blessed when they help the poor. Taking action is necessary when being generous. Most everyone can look around and see that there are people in need. But it's what the individual does when he or she sees the need that determines his or her generosity.

Text: 2 Kings 4:8–17

Seek and Find

- 2 Kings 4:8
  How is the Shunamite woman described in this Scripture?

- 2 Kings 4:8
  What did the Shunamite woman do for Elisha, the man of God?

- 2 Kings 4:8
  Did Elisha come to this woman's house again for food?

- 2 Kings 4:9–10
  The Shunamite woman noticed that Elisha was a godly man. She also noticed that he was in need of something. What was Elisha in need of?

- 2 Kings 4:11
  What did Elisha do when he came to her house the next time he was in town?

Elisha wanted to show his gratitude to this woman for her generosity. Gehazi, his servant, asked her what she wanted. She responded that she was content with what she had. Gehazi noticed that she didn't have a child. He made this information known to Elisha.

- 2 Kings 4:16
  How did Elisha bless the Shunamite woman?

Think about It

Circle the correct answer below.

2 Kings 4:8

God had put it on this woman's heart to provide a simple meal for Elisha. The Scripture tells us that she went out and found Elisha. Then she begged him to come eat at her house. From this we can learn:

    a.   you must wait for someone to approach you before you help them.

    b.   you need to be looking for ways to serve others.

2 Kings 4:9

The Shunamite woman was involved in her community. We know this because she was able to determine that Elisha was a traveler who passed through on a regular basis. Her knowledge of the people who surrounded her tells us what type of person she was:

    a.   selfless

    b.   self-absorbed

2 Kings 4:9

Elisha was a stranger to the woman. She could have looked the other way when she saw his need. She could have told herself that there were other people within the community with a better financial situation, but she didn't. Also, she didn't let the fact that she would only encounter Elisha occasionally deter her from serving him. From this we can learn:

a. A few acts of service can affect a person's life.
b. People are only affected if they are served over a long period of time.

2 Kings 4:10

We read that the Shunamite woman and her husband built a small room for Elisha to stay in when he passed through Shunem. They didn't build him a "guest suite." Why do you think that was?

a. They only wanted to give enough to say that they did it.
b. They were staying within their financial means.

2 Kings 4:10

The Shunamite woman went out of her way to make Elisha comfortable. In addition to the bed in the room, she also provided him with a table, stool, and candle. Based on her extra effort given to make the room welcoming, we see that little things:

a. are a waste of time and money.
b. make a difference in making a person not feel like a burden.

2 Kings 4:11

Elisha chose to stay in the bedroom that they had prepared for him. What does this tell us about the atmosphere in which he ate the meals she had prepared for him?

    a.   It was hostile, full of tension, and unwelcoming.
    b.   It was peaceful, relaxed, and welcoming.

At the beginning of this study, we learned that there are benefits to being humble. Had the Shunamite woman not invited Elisha into her home, Gehazi, Elisha's servant, wouldn't have seen that she was without child. Therefore, Elisha wouldn't have blessed her with a son.

True or False: Servanthood only benefits the person being served.

Wrapping It Up

The Shunamite woman was only able to serve Elisha when he would occasionally pass through her town. However, she didn't allow the number of opportunities to deter her from serving him. Nor did she let the lack of abundant finances stop her from providing him food and lodging at her own expense. In her humility, she was blessed not only with a friend but with a long-awaited child.

Lesson 15

Servanthood isn't just limited to an act. It can be a lifestyle. Today we are going to study Ruth and the lifestyle choice she made that forever affected her mother-in-law and herself.

Text: Ruth chapters 1–2

Seek and Find

- Ruth 1:1
  Naomi, her husband, and her two sons left their home country for what reason?

- Ruth 1:2
  What country did they move to?

- Ruth 1:3
  What happened to Naomi's husband?

- Ruth 1:4
  What were the names of Naomi's daughters-in-law?

- Ruth 1:5
  What happened to Ruth's husband and brother-in-law?

- Ruth 1:16–17
  Ruth told Naomi that she wanted to do what?

- Ruth 1:22

  What did Ruth and Naomi do next?

- Ruth 2:2

  How did Ruth plan to provide for Naomi and herself?

- Ruth 2:3

  Upon whose part of the field did she reap?

- Ruth 2:8

  Did Ruth find favor in Boaz's eyes?

- Ruth 4:13

  Ruth and Boaz later became what?

- Ruth 4:17

  What did they name their son?

- Ruth 4:22

  Obed was grandfather to whom?

Think about It

Circle the correct answer below.

- Ruth 1:5

  Naomi had come upon a hard time in her life. It had been over ten years since she, her husband, and their two sons had left Bethlehem for Moab. Naomi found herself a widow past the childbearing stage and too old to remarry. Her sons' death only worsened her state. Now there wasn't anyone left to provide for her financially. Ruth, a recent widow herself, took her mother-in-law's situation into consideration. She then made the life-altering decision to devote her life to Naomi. She chose to leave her family, culture, and gods to serve Naomi. She chose to take Naomi as her family, to conform to her culture, and to serve her God. In doing so, she would live a lifestyle of humility. What type of thought process probably reigned in Ruth's mind?

  a. Maybe she has a rich relative back home I can marry.

  b. She needs me, and I am capable of providing for her.

- Ruth 2:11

  Ruth worked day in and day out to provide for Naomi and herself. She was in the fields when the day began until the workday ended. Boaz, owner of the fields that she gleaned from, took notice of her. He told his workers to leave extra for her to pick up. He also gave her food to eat and water to drink. She had found favor in his sight. He found her favorable because he saw the humility she had shown to her mother-in-law. Our humble acts will always be rewarded. Sometimes the reward is just between you and Jesus, but

sometimes He'll bring in someone else to bless you here on earth. Ruth's blessing teaches us:
   a. earthly blessings should be appreciated and viewed as a gift from God.
   b. we should turn away from another's generosity.

- Ruth 4:15

   Ruth was blessed immensely because of the sacrifice she made for her mother-in-law day after day. Can you imagine if she would have chosen not to take part in Naomi's life after the deaths? Her entire life would have been different, and so would have Naomi's. Often the sacrifice we make to serve another is a big decision. It seems to me that the greater the sacrifice, the more powerful the reward for all involved.

   What had Ruth sacrificed?

   What did she gain?

- Matthew 1:5

   Ruth was able to leave a legacy that will have her recorded forever in God's Word. She will always be known as part of the family of Jesus. Humility offers us that same relationship. When we humble ourselves and accept Jesus as our Lord and Savior, we become part of Christ's family.

Wrapping It Up

Ruth chose to give of herself to Naomi. She made the decision to be there for Naomi on a daily basis in several different ways. Living a servant's life wasn't torture for her. Instead, it was the beginning of blessings.

LESSON 16

Review of the Facts

Matching

How often did Philip serve the Ethiopian treasurer?	Daily
How often did the Shunamite woman serve Elisha?	Once
How often did Ruth serve Naomi?	Occasionally

Matching

What did Ruth offer?	Time
What did Philip provide?	Finances
What did the Shunamite woman serve?	Self

Making It Applicable

How have you served others before?

Is there a person or group of people that the Lord has encouraged you to serve? How often would you have the opportunity to serve them?

In what ways do you or would you enjoy serving people?

Do you look for opportunities to serve others?

How has the Lord blessed you when you have had a servant's heart?

MEETING 4

- Open in prayer.
- Discuss *Review of the Facts* from Lesson 16.
- Read or summarize *Cold Feet*.

Isn't that just like Jesus? He takes little happenings and reveals Himself to His children. In this instance, I learned that there isn't any act of service that is considered too small in God's eyes. Sure, cozy feet aren't necessary, but a willing heart is. That type of heart is exactly what my daughter had when Jesus nudged her to become a servant to her sister. That's what He asks of us, too. He wants His children to be willing to serve in whatever capacity or frequency He asks. He'll bless us for it.

Open up discussion between you, God, and your brothers and sisters in Christ.

- Share times when others have served you.
- Discuss ways that you, as a group, could serve others.

I want to thank you for taking the time to complete this study on humility. I trust that Jesus has spoken to your heart, drawing you closer to Him. I want to remind you that you have been chosen to be a vessel for Christ. The Word teaches us that we are all capable of being humble. It shows us how to be humble, when to be humble, and why we should be humble. You have the pieces of the puzzle laid out before you. But remember that Jesus is the one who puts the pieces together. He is the one who has given you the desire to be humble. He is the author of the humble word you speak or humble action you take. It is Jesus who provides you with opportunities to humble yourself before humans, before Him. Take heed that you don't become prideful in your humility, because even your humbleness is a gift from God. Without Jesus, our acts of righteousness are as filthy rags, but with Him, they are as white as snow. To God be the glory.

- Encourage one another.
- Praise God.
- Close in prayer.